By Rose & Frank Winn

The Adventures of Rose Bud

The Great Escape

Illustrated by usillustrations.com

2023

A wonderful story! This is the third book of three. The Adventures of Rose Bud, born with a rose over her heart and her quest to find her missing dad, is filled with adventure, hope, and the power of friendship. Rose Bud's determination to find her dad takes her on many exciting adventures. She discovers that the rose over her heart is not only beautiful but is very special. Rose Bud's message to everyone is, "Let's be friends."

@2023 Rose Winn & Frank Winn

www.rosemariebud.store

ISBN

All rights reserved.

Dedicated to my mother and Rose's Nana. A woman who had many special gifts and will always be our biggest fan.

While searching for her missing dad,
Rose Bud had fallen deep into a dark hole.
A voice from above yelled down and asked,
"Hey, are you all right down there?"
"Yes," Rose Bud replied with her voice faint.
"If you are able to, flap your wings
as hard as you can and fly straight up!"
With all her might, Rose Bud started flapping
her wings and she began to fly. Like a rocket,
she shot up and out of the hole.

"Hi, my name is Rose Bud. I'm glad you found me.
I was so scared I almost forgot that I could fly."
"Hi Rose Bud, my name is Jack. I saw you fall in that hole
and I was hoping you were not hurt. I am on my way
to search for a ladybug I was told is in trouble."
"That is quite a coincidence," Rose Bud said.
"I am looking for my dad. He may also be in trouble.
Maybe, we can go together."
Jack nodded and agreed. Rose Bud took Jack's hand
and said, "Let's be friends."

Rose Bud and Jack walked until they came upon a beautiful path in the woods. They were quickly becoming friends.

Rose Bud's curiosity got the best of her. She turned to Jack and asked, "So why do they call you Jack, anyway?"

"They call me Jack because I was born with a 'J' over my heart," he said proudly.

"That is so funny," Rose Bud giggled. "That is how I got my name. I was born with a rose over my heart."

They both laughed and began to dance.

Jack said, "This place is very beautiful Rose Bud. Almost as beautiful as you and your pretty flower." Rose Bud blushed and the two of them continued to dance.

Rose Bud and Jack came upon a river crossing. Rose Bud said to Jack, "Let's hold hands and cross the river together."

Suddenly, Rose Bud slipped and fell into the water.
In a panic, Jack tried to save her.

Magically, Rose Bud was lifted up in the air
by a crazy-looking reptile wearing nothing more
than a snorkel and some scuba fins.

"Chick!" Rose Bud screamed with excitement.
"Is that really you?!"
"I thought I lost you forever," she cried.
"The last time I saw you, you were wrestling with a
hippopotamus and you both fell over a waterfall."

"It's all me!" Chick boasted, as he chuckled
and shook his long scaly tail.
Rose Bud was so happy to be reunited with her friend.
She introduced Chick to Jack and told him about
their plan to continue their search for her dad
and a ladybug Jack said may be in trouble.

Chick offered his help and invited them
to ride on his back.

The clouds started to darken and it started to rain.
Quickly, Chick swam up to a nearby island.
"It's getting late and we should find shelter for the night and continue our search in the morning," Chick said.
Rose Bud and Jack both agreed.

The next day, the three of them continued their search until they came upon a dark spooky cave.
"This is really creepy," Rose Bud whispered.
Jack and Chick stared deeply into the dark cave.

"Look!" Rose Bud shrieked. "It's my dad!"

"Oh my," said Jack. "It looks like your dad may be the same ladybug I was told is in trouble."

"We need to be quiet," cautioned Chick. "I'm afraid that whoever has your dad trapped could be nearby."

All at once, the three of them let out a loud gasp! A giant spider appeared and she was hovering around Rose Bud's dad.

"We need to do something," cried Rose Bud.
"We have to rescue my dad!"
Jack agreed but said with hesitation, "This looks impossible. That spider is watching your dad very closely."
Chick thought for a second and said with confidence, "I have a plan."

Chick grabbed some leaves and stuck two sticks on top of his head. He yelled to the spider and started singing and dancing. "Ladybug, ladybug, look at me, I'm bright and beautiful so come after me!"

Quick as a flash, Rose Bud and Jack grabbed
her dad and they started to run.
Unfortunately, they didn't get very far.
The mean old spider had figured out their plan
and spun a web around them.

The spider showed her fangs and with a loud hiss, said, "Now that I have all of you in my web, I'm going to keep you here forever!"

"Oh, please Madam Spider. Please let us go," Rose Bud begged.
"I finally found my dad; I only want to bring him home. My mother, brothers and sisters are waiting for us to return. We just want to be together as a family."

The spider gazed at Rose Bud with her scary green eyes
as if she did not understand. Then she said impatiently,
"First of all, my name is not Madame Spider.
My name is Penny! I am moved by your desire
to be with your family but I can not let you go."

Suddenly, baby spiders started crawling out from inside the dark cave.
They all started hissing and begging their mother, "Mommy, Mommy, please let them go. They just want to be a family. They want to just be like us."

Penny looked at her children and you could see that she loved them very much.

"Penny," Rose Bud said, "I was born with a rose over my heart and I have learned it is always better to make friends than enemies. Can't we just be friends?"

Penny gazed at Rose Bud and the beautiful
flower over Rose Bud's heart.
She could feel the kindness and the power of her rose.
Penny calmed down, shrugged her shoulders, and said,
"What the Hay! Let's all be friends! I want to introduce
you to my children. Brittany, Johnny, Jessica, Joe, CJ,
Zach, Josh, Nina, Ashley, Brianna, Charles, Colton,
Maddox, Andi, Griffey, Olivia, Gilbert and Charlee."
Everyone cheered!

Rose Bud thanked Penny and all her children
as the four of them waved goodbye.
Rose Bud and her dad were finally going home.

The next day they arrived to a big celebration!

Rose Bud's mom was so excited upon their arrival, she ran up to Rose Bud's dad and shouted out, "Frank, you are home!"

"Frank?" Rose Bud asked, with a surprise look on her face.

"Yes. I'm your dad, Frank. I am so proud of you Rose Bud, and because of you and your friends, we are all home together as a family. I love you all!"

Everyone was so happy and they all gathered at the leaf house.
And... as the story goes.
They all lived happily ever after.

The End

Scan Me

Rose Winn is a student at Full Sail University, where she is pursuing a degree in the Arts. She attended school in Fernandina Beach and Douglas Anderson School of Arts, where she began her journey. She has directed numerous productions in her community and is thrilled to add an Author to her list of talents. Working with her father Frank has been a blast and she hopes kids all over the world will enjoy "The Adventures of Rose Bud!"

Frank Winn was born in Yonkers, New York, one of six children. He is married to his wife Kathleen and their daughter is Rose Marie Winn. Frank is currently a resident of Fernandina Beach, Florida, and has spent 40 years working in Aerospace, Aviation, and Defense businesses. During this time, he worked as a Manager for the Space Shuttle Program. Frank invented "The Invisible Jump Rope" in 1992. He is currently working part-time as a business assessor and loves spending time writing children's books with his daughter Rose (aka Rose Bud).